T0078396

Unwritten Love

MEMOIRS OF CAPE TOWN

UNA DIRKSE

authorHOUSE®

AuthorHouse™
1663 Liberty Drive
Bloomington, IN 47403
www.authorhouse.com
Phone: 833-262-8899

Published by AuthorHouse 12/11/2020

ISBN: 978-1-6655-0828-5 (sc)
ISBN: 978-1-6655-0827-8 (e)

Library of Congress Control Number: 2020923120

Print information available on the last page.

INTRODUCTION

I was born in Cape Town, South Africa during Apartheid. I was classified as "Coloured" because; in our country we were separated into different race groups, such as Black, White, Coloured and Indian. The Coloured people were descendants of the Khoisan people (Bushman). We go way back to 1652 when the Dutch East India Company landed at the Cape of Good Hope and established a trading colony in Kaapstad, later known as Cape Town. South Africa, during Apartheid, was a police state designed to keep different race groups under control. There were also Chinese people who were classified as "Black" and Japanese who were classified as "White". This never made sense to me until later. I learned that South Africa had to establish a relationship with Japan, because they needed their help importing cars and electronics in the country. Due to the resources and support Japan provided to South Africa, the Japanese people were given honorary White status. On the other hand, although the Chinese people were considered Black and had lived in my Coloured area, they were eligible to attend White only schools, while I, was still restricted to Coloured only schools.

When the Dutch landed in Cape Town, they encountered the Khoisan people who were the indigenous people of the land. The White colonist had sexual relations with the Khoisan women; this is how the first mixed people of South Africa were born; later to be classified as Coloured citizens. Over time the Khoisan people were continued to be exploited by the White colonist and the slaves, whom they imported from different corners of the Dutch Empire. The Khoisan and the slaves married, which resulted in a new race of people. Some of these new races of people were light skinned, some looked Asian, while others had White and/or Black features. Coloured people do not speak African languages; we speak English and Afrikaans. All the things that shaped our culture came from the Afrikaners. In South Africa, Coloured people at the time were second class citizens, who were denied the rights of White people, but were given special privileges that Black people did not have. Every year, Coloured people could have themselves reclassified as White, if their skin colour was white enough or hair was straight enough. All they had to do, was denounce their history and leave their dark-skinned friends and family behind. My husband, used to work for a White employer, who we later learned was Coloured, but he had applied and was approved to be reclassified as White. Unfortunately, his siblings did not qualify, because of their skin tone. He had to leave them behind and separate from his family to live his life as a White person. Sad as it may seem, there were many cases like this back then. There were also cases, where Black and Indian people applied to get reclassified as Coloured. At the end of the day, it all came down to skin colour. This is what shaped our lives in South Africa during Apartheid.

DEDICATIONS

This book is dedicated to all the grandparents, who are left with the responsibility of raising their grandchildren in cases where, the parents have died, or where the parents just left. A special thanks to my grandmother (Wilhelmina McDuma); whose unselfish love for her five granddaughters sparked me to write this book. You are the real "Hero" of our time. I salute you!!

CONTENTS

CHAPTER 1

The Rock

I can clearly remember my grandmother (Wilhelmina McDuma), taking my siblings and I to the dressmaker across the road; she had us fitted with white dresses. I also remember her going to the Chinese variety store down the road to buy us black ribbons for our hair. This is what we would wear to our mother's funeral, white dresses and black ribbons in our hair.

Being so young, we did not quite understand what funerals meant; my sisters and I were more excited about our new outfits. At the time, I was ten years old, my sister Dandeleen was eight, Jeanette six, Daphne three, and our baby sister Joyce was only one-day old. Our mother (Joyce Anthony) died the day after giving birth to my baby sister, who was named after her. Mom suffered of hypertension and hemorrhaged after birth. In those days, women would give birth to their first child at the hospital, in case of an emergency. After their first child they were required to give birth to additional babies at home, with the help of a midwife. My baby sister was born on a Friday and Mom died the next day (Saturday). The ambulance was summoned, and the Paramedics frantically tried to save her life, but were too late. The baby was placed in a separate bedroom with my Dad (Christoffel Anthony) who wept bitterly. At the time, there were two midwives who served our area; they were Nurse Lawrence and Nurse Wiegeman. I cannot remember exactly which nurse was assigned to my Mom, but I do remember how devastated she was at the loss of her patient.

After Mom was certified dead, the neighbours and family came over to pay their respects. Some were somber, some were crying, some were whaling, and others offered prayers and hymns. As a custom among the Coloured people, some brought cookies and tea, to be served to the mourners. In between the mourners would recite Psalm 23 "The Lord is my Sheppard", which I later learnt was also known as the "Psalm of death". Mom's body was washed and covered with a white sheet; she remained on her bed for the next three days. In those days (year 1962) either mortuary costs were too expensive for my Dad to afford, or they just did not exist. On the day of the funeral, the undertakers came to our home, placed her in the coffin and drove her to church for the funeral service. The church was called N.G. Kerk; it was a Dutch reformed church located on Banjo Street Steenberg, which was the same street where we lived at the time. This church was newly built in our area and was mainly to serve the Coloured parishioners of the church. Grandma, sat in the front pew, with her granddaughters sitting beside her; all girls dressed in white dresses and black ribbons in their hair. She was holding baby Joyce, who was wrapped in a white shawl in her arms. She was burying her eldest daughter who was only 33 years old.

Banjo Street Steenberg, is in the Western Cape of South Africa. We were the first to move into this area, which was strategically built for Coloured people. This was part of the government group, areas planned to keep different races apart. Despite of the situation and events going on in the area, my parents at the time were simply happy to have their own home and space. Prior to having my parent's own home, they had to share a house with my Dad's family, who then lived on 9th Avenue Retreat.

After Mom's burial, we went to our Grandma's house; this was where we planned to live and spend the rest of our young lives. I must mention that our baby sister was deeply loved, nurtured and spoiled by our grandmother, whom we lovingly referred to as "Ma" and who would now become our guardian. Our Dad, who loved us very dearly, would not have been able to raise us as a single Dad. I believe if Ma were not around, we would probably have been split up into foster homes, or with different family members but not in the same home with a loving environment. At the time of Mom's death, our Ma had just finished raising her six children of whom the youngest was an eighteen-year-old. Just as she thought that it was time for her to relax, she started all over again, with now having to raise her five granddaughters.

Ma was illiterate; she supported the family by working as a domestic servant for a white family. Knowing Ma's predicament, her employer Mrs. De Bruin, was a wonderful woman who would often go out of her way to help Ma care for us. Sometimes Mrs. De Bruin, would go shopping and buy us some gifts. I would meet up with her to pick up the gifts on Wynberg Station. The gifts would include new underwear, socks, and sometimes new shoes for me, which I had to try on at the station. Although I was excited and grateful for my new shoes, I was also embarrassed, when people use to stare at us. After our meeting at the station, I would get a hug and we would part ways. I loved Mrs. De Bruin, for how she spoiled us. When Ma used to come home after work, we would be excited to see what Mrs. De Bruin had sent for us, in the form of candy. I also remember going to work with Ma; while she cleaned the house, I got the chance to play with her pets. She had a Parrot who could only say "hello and goodbye"; she also had a Siamese cat, whom I loved very much and a Shiatsu puppy.

While our Ma took on all these responsibilities, our grandpa, whom we lovingly referred to as "Pa" continued to work as the Head Chef at the Blue Moon Hotel in Lakeside. He loved us very dearly and although he was not our biological grandpa, his love for us never altered. These are two people in my life, whom I absolutely adored and who taught me values and help shape who I am today. We do not know our biological grandfather, but with Pa in our lives, we had the best. I can truly say "hooray" to grandparents.

Every life's journey ends in death. I would like to think, that life is a long preparation for that moment; yet our Mom did not even get the chance to say "good-bye". She was 33 years old at the time of her death. We all must die, but it is always sad that some must go sooner than others. The day when Ma and Pa heard that their eldest daughter had died, it must have been the worst day of their lives. Anyone who had lost a child, will understand how lonely the experience can be. However, the more you are surrounded by family, friends, neighbors, the easier it becomes to digest and go through. I can honestly say that Ma and Pa (Wilhelmina McDuma and Daniel Joel McDuma Sr) were "The Rock" in our lives.

Wilhelmina and Daniel Joel McDuma
Sr 1967 (Ma and Pa)

CHAPTER 2

Church Bells

As I mentioned at the time of Mom's passing, we lived in Steenberg in a council dwelling, which was newly built for the Coloured race. It was a semi-detached home with two bedrooms, a kitchen, bathroom, living room, with a large front yard and backyard. Our neighbours did not get along well with Mom; they barely looked at each other. Our Dad earned just enough to pay the weekly rent and to buy food for the week. Mom went through daily struggles to support us. Mom would stitch our dresses by hand and used recycled materials. She was a master when it came to having to make ends meet. Our house was always spotlessly clean. Since at a young age, she taught my younger sister Dandeleen and I how to keep our bedroom clean and tidy; she taught us how to complete chores before going out to play.

Friday nights were set aside for house cleaning. It was also the night when my Dad would come home intoxicated after getting paid. On his way home, he would first stop at the bottle store, then have a drink with his friends. He would also buy us fruits and chocolate. He gave my Mom what was left of his pay after that. My Dad used to argue a lot when he was intoxicated, especially Friday nights. After arguing about money, Mom would carefully bury the rent money, which at the time cost twelve shillings and six pence a week. At that time, the country still used British currency. In order to save us from eviction, she would rather pay her rent first and then budget for food. Towards the end of the week, there would be no more cash for food; we survived on cereal for breakfast, lunch, and dinner. When Dad was sober, he was the best. I loved him when he was sober but hated him when he was not. There were times when he would beat me for no reason; it was normal for parents to discipline their kids this way, it was accepted back then. Many times, Mom would get in between, but would then, be the one to get the blows. If Dad had a valid reason to punish me, I could understand, but I guess in his drunken state, he was not fully aware of his actions.

Dad and our grandma (Mom's Mom) did not care for one another. After we moved to grandma's house, Dad was evicted from his house and had to move back to his Dad's residence on 9th Avenue Retreat. Although we now lived at least forty minutes away from him, he would come and see us every night after work. Whenever he was intoxicated, he would argue with grandma. Now and again, he would give her money towards our up-bringing. Dad never owned a car; he never even had a driver's license. When he dated my Mom, they would get around using his bicycle. I have a picture of my Mom, proudly show casing his bike. My

Dad was very fit; he walked around a lot during his days; I remember he would do forty-minute walks to the train station in the morning and at night.

My Dad's family was well known in their neighbourhood (Avenue Retreat). His father (my grandfather) was Mr. Anthony; he owned a huge piece of property on the corner of Retreat Road and 9th Avenue Retreat. He named his property "Springfield", which was well known in the area. I do not remember my grandmother (Dad's Mom), because she passed when I was incredibly young. But I do remember Dad's Dad very well. I lovingly referred to him as "Oupa Anthony". Before we moved to Banjo Street, we lived with him, until I was about six years old. Oupa Anthony used to call me "his little Una". Oupa Anthony used to grow his own vegetables on his property. He had chickens running around freely; he also gave me cats and a bulldog to take care of and play with. My dog's name was Bonzo. At the time when I obtained Bonzo, he was already considered old in dog years. Bonzo was either old and overweight, or lazy and overweight. Nevertheless, I wanted to treat Bonzo as if he were a playful puppy, but when that did not work, I would just ride on his back. Every night my Dad would cook Bonzo's food, which would consist of leftovers mixed in with mielie meal. Oupa Anthony grew carrots, potatoes, corn, onions, peas, herbs, pumpkin and strawberries on his property. My favourite were the sweet strawberries, and sweet baby peas. Living with Oupa Anthony got us used to eating organic vegetables and free-range chickens. My Dad (Christoffel Anthony) was the youngest son; it was clear that Dad absolutely admired his father.

Oupa Anthony, used to ring the church bells on Sunday mornings and nights at the N.G. Kerk (Dutch reformed church), which was in Tokai. Later, that specific location was reclassified as a "Whites" only area, therefore the church had to relocate to an acceptable area for the Coloured people. The new location was farther from where we lived. Oupa Anthony, used to walk about an hour to get to church and back. He did this twice on Sundays, for the morning service and then for the evening service. I remember being so proud of him. As a six-year-old, if your grandfather is the person who oversees ringing the church bells, you would think the world of him. I remember when he used to get ready for church; he always wore a suit and tie, and he would shine up his shoes with black polish. He would also run the shoe polish brush over his hair to cover the gray. I tried doing that one day and got into trouble, because Mom had to wash my hair because it reeked of shoe polish. Oupa Anthony was the most important man to me at that time, because he had to make sure that the church bells rang.

Occasionally my Dad would take me and Dandeleen to church with Oupa Anthony. What bothered me most when we went was the fact that we had to sit at the back of the church, even though the church was half empty. When I asked my Dad why we do not sit in front, he would be very vague and tell me, that I would not understand, and should not ask so many questions. I felt that we should be getting the front seats, because if it were not for Oupa Anthony, those bells would not be ringing. Later as I was growing up, my Mom explained to me that the front rows of the church were reserved for White people only, and the back rows were for the Coloured people. At such a young age, that feeling of inferiority was already instilled in us. I also learned that the N.G. Kerk (Dutch reformed church) and all other denominations had to apply a rule, whereby which, White people, sit in front and other races at the back.

My Dad was Oupa Anthony's youngest son. I was young when Ouma Anthony (Dad's Mom) died therefore, did not have vivid memories of her. My Dad had many siblings, of which I only remember a handful of them. When Mom died, we had little to no contact with Dad's side of the family. In fact, I only met one of my Dad's brothers for the first time at my Dad's funeral, about thirty years later; his name was Uncle Daan. When we met, Uncle Dan apologized for not being in our lives after Mom passed away. I was already 38 years old at that time and became emotional at the thought that I could have passed him by on the street, not knowing that he was my uncle. The Anthony's are a big family, but I only knew a few relatives from that side. I never had the chance to meet and got to know my cousins from that side. Oupa Anthony died about a year after Mom; I have only fond memories of him. My Dad was devastated when his father died. He used to visit us at Ma's house and when he was in a sober state, he would reminisce about his late father. I think he absolutely adored his Dad and having lost him, left a huge void especially so soon after Mom. I wish I knew more about Ouma Anthony (Dad's Mom), but I did not ask about her, and Dad never used to talk much about her either. However, I was told that she was a beautiful lady who had more White genes, whereas Oupa Anthony had more black genes. My Dad looked more like Oupa Anthony, medium height, well-built, olive complexion, thick curly hair and upright when sober.

Three years after Mom died, Dad remarried. Our stepmother, whom we lovingly referred to as "Aunty Maggie" was a wonderful stepmom. She embraced us as if we were her own. When she married my Dad, she made sure that he paid my Ma regularly to provide for us. Prior to that, Dad would just pay Ma when he felt like it. Aunty Maggie's love for us was genuine and although Grandma did not care for her at first, they compromised for our well-being. I remember Ma telling us never to call Aunty Maggie "Mom", as she was not our Mom and will never be able to replace her. Aunty Maggie became part of our lives till many years after our father died. She was a few years older than him but outlived him. Aunty Maggie worked at a candy factory known as "Humphries". On a Friday, she would bring us chocolates. I particularly remember during Christmas and Easter time; the top of our piano would always be covered in chocolate eggs. My Dad and Aunty Maggie continued to live at Oupa Anthony's house after he passed away. Sadly, the house caught on fire and burnt down while my Dad and Aunty Maggie was still living in it. The children decided to sell the property and split the money. Today, there is a church and three houses on the property, which Oupa Anthony was so proud of. "Springfield" and "9th Avenue Retreat" will always remind me of Oupa Anthony and his love for me.

My dad Christoffel Anthony on my wedding day 1975

CHAPTER 3

A Very Special Day

My memorable day in Ma's house was on a Sunday but started on a Saturday night. When my sisters and I moved into Ma's house, five of her adult children were still living with her. My aunts and uncles (Connie, Veronica, Sarah, Dan, and John) would now be sharing their home with their five nieces. At that time kids would live with their parents, until they got married or decide to move out on their own. With all Ma's children, grandchildren and two boarders, we had a total count of sixteen people who lived in Ma's house. Our uncles and aunts accepted us and played a role in caring for us. On Saturday nights, we had to help prepare the meal for Sunday lunch, when the whole family would gather to bond and to enjoy, what looked like a feast. Grandpa was the one who would say grace before the meal. He took his time saying grace; from a kid's point of view, it always seemed like it was never going to end because it was so long. Meanwhile, I would be eyeballing a single chicken in the centre of the table that did not appear, as if it could provide for sixteen people.

There were plenty of rice, vegetables, roast potatoes, and a pot of hot gravy. After Ma dished for the kids we ended up with a plate of rice and vegetables, gravy and a sliver of chicken. The adults would consume the better part of the chicken. My favorite part of the chicken was the tail end (parson's nose) and this would become my share. Ma had a best friend, Aunty Annie, who was also raising her six grandchildren and was also in the same situation as Ma. Every so often Aunty Annie would show up, unexpectedly with her six grandchildren, on a Sunday at lunch time. Our Ma would welcome her and assure the family that we had more than plenty to provide and she was always right. At the end of lunch there would still be leftovers. The only thing I hated about Aunty Annie's visit was the fact that her favorite part of the chicken was also the tail end; therefore, my share of chicken went to Aunty Annie. Desert options would always be jelly, custard, bread pudding, rice pudding, and cake for afternoon tea. On Sunday nights, Ma would cook a pot of soup which we could consume with bread. Ma had a coal stove in her kitchen which also created a welcoming atmosphere. Her house was always open to visitors and they always felt welcome. On Sunday mornings we had to dress in our church clothes; the outfits would include a bag, gloves, hat and bobby socks. By this time Ma took us out of the Dutch Reformed Church and sent us to the Anglican Church where she was a member. This was something that my Dad resented because she did so without his consent. Saint Cyprians Anglican Church at Retreat Station was where we would worship and be confirmed in. This is also a church which had to re-locate due to the group areas act and moved to the Coloured area in Retreat. The Anglican Church also had to abide by the government rules, but according to Ma, her church was more laidback in the sense that they only allocated the two front rows for Whites-only. In fact, the two rows were sufficient for the few White folks who attended on a Sunday. Coming home from church we had to change our clothing and got ready for lunch which was always at 1 p.m.

My Pa (Mom's Dad) was the person I always looked up to. Although my Dad used to see us every day after work, my Pa was the one who was influential in our lives. He was a tall, up right, and well-dressed gentleman, with a very dark skin tone and possibly strong black roots. Pa was very well educated with good knowledge of the bible. He also had keen interest in politics especially the A.N.C. (African National Congress) which was a resistance movement. The A.N.C. was set to oppose the White minority government and thereby set the Black people free. The A.N.C. did not only consist of Black members, but all those who believed in the struggle against Apartheid. The A.N.C. won the 1994 election and Nelson Mandela became the President. My Pa was well respected in the community because of the way he carried himself. He could walk into a crowded room and get attention without saying anything. While Ma attended the Anglican Church, Pa was a member of The New Apostolic Church to which he was very devoted. Ever so now and again Pa would try to get us to attend his church, but Ma would quickly intervene. I can truly say that I had two grandfathers whom I absolutely admired and adored. On Sundays after lunch, we would visit our Mom's gravesite with Ma and then get ready for family worship on Sunday night.

CHAPTER 4

Bucket and Spade

As I mentioned before, I think my Mom was Grandma's favorite child. I think this, because she would often visit her at the cemetery on Sundays, after lunch; she missed her daughter very much. We lived in Heathfield, but the cemetery was in Grassy Park. It was not within walking distance, but one bus ride away. In those years, very few people owned a car. The only person I can think of that owned a car was Uncle John, but his car was often broken. Ma never relied on a car and would often use public transportation when needed. Every Sunday, after lunch we would dress in our Sunday best and get ready for our visit to the cemetery. Our baby sister Joyce was still too small to go, so one of our aunts would always babysit her. The visit to the cemetery would always include a walk to the bus stop with a bucket and spade. On our way we would stop at Mrs. Basson's house for flowers. Mrs. Basson had a flower garden consisting of wildflowers and perennials, which she would sell to Ma at 10 cents a bunch. I think she sold it to

Ma at a special price knowing that it was for Mom's grave site. I loved Mrs. Basson because I always remember my Mom stopping there for a chat. She would always be invited in for tea and there would always be scones and cheese or freshly baked cookies. She was immensely proud of her house which was built for her by her employer whom she worked for as a domestic maid. She was especially proud of her flower garden, vegetables and herbs. After getting the flowers we would walk to the bus stop with bucket and spade and flowers in hand. When I was about ten this did not bother me too much, but later, I found it embarrassing to be walking with a bucket and spade, especially when I met my friends along the way. I think Ma also used the cemetery as our weekly social outing. Once we got off the bus at Grassy Park, we had to do a fifteen-minute walk to the cemetery. At Mom's gravesite, Ma would first talk to our late Mom, which my younger siblings found very disturbing. My middle sister Janet (Jeanette) who was only six at the time would look at me and say, "Una who is Ma talking to, I don't like this, I want to go home". Janet would walk away after our little chat about Ma's conversation with Mom; she would start walking towards the cemetery gate. I would run after her and try to convince her that it was okay. Ma's conversation with our late Mom would go like this "Joyce, I am here with all your children. Una is doing wonderful at school. She is taking ballet lessons and at the school concert, she took the leading role in a dance segment. Dandeleen, is still running from one mirror to another. She is very precise on her appearance which is a good thing. I think she takes after you. Now Janet gives me a lot of problems with her hair. After I braided her hair, she would undo the braids, run around in the street and come home with bushy hair. I think she loves having the wind blow through her hair. Now Daphne is still so sweet. Everybody loves her. She has become Connie's child and I am happy that Connie is taking full responsibility for her well -being." There would always be an update on our baby sister, who was also named Joyce, the same as our mother. After we cared for Mom's grave, we would visit Ma sister's gravesite nearby and placed what was left of the flowers on it. Ma's conversation with her sister would go like this "Lizzie, in life you were very untidy and look at you now, I can't even get the weeds out with a spade. Even in death you are still the same". Whenever she said that, she would have a little chuckle afterwards. After having spent about an hour at the cemetery we would make our way home, but not before saying goodbye to Mom. Along the way we would stop at the shop for candy and ice suckers. The cemetery will always have a special place in my memory because this was every Sunday, with bucket and spade in hand.

CHAPTER 5

Family Time

Back in those days almost every family had a piano. My Aunt Sarah used to play the piano; as a child she took piano lessons. Ma was proud of her daughter Sarah because she also played the organ in church. My Dad, Uncle Dan, and Uncle John could also play, they were all self-taught. Uncle Dan would play jazzy tunes. Uncle John, commonly known as "Uncle Gawie" would play his favorite tunes, but when I would listen to him play, even as a child, I could tell he was always out of tune. If that was not enough, Uncle John also attempted to play the piano accordion. I would say that his attempt at the latter was worse. He would play and sing as false as he played. It was painful to listen to him. Grandpa would gather the family together on Sunday nights, after we had our soup and bread for dinner. Aunt Sarah would be at the piano and we would gather for prayers, scripture reading, and hymn singing. As always, it seemed as if Grandpa's prayers would never end. Even Ma would quietly remind him to end his prayer. Uncle

John would even jump in when he had enough, he would sarcastically say "amen Daddy amen" while grandpa is still in deep devotion. After the gathering Ma would proceed to prepare the work and school lunches for the next day. Every now and then on Sundays, one of my aunts would bake fresh bread for the next day (Monday), because it was usually hard to find fresh bread at the store on Mondays. Ma would slice three loaves of bread a day for family work and school lunches. Unlike today, sliced bread was not yet available. Occasionally Uncle John would grab his piano accordion and while Ma is preparing the lunches, he would walk around the kitchen table and aggravate her with his music. She would eventually stop what she was doing and chase him out of her kitchen. Uncle John's favorite song was "Please Release Me" by Engelbert Humperdinck; he also enjoyed certain songs by Tom Jones. Even today whenever I hear Uncle John's favorite song on the radio, I still get a chuckle. I can say that Sundays for us was a feast, celebration, devotion, family time and yes, a lot of love.

Aunt Sarah in Middle with Me far right
and Dandeline far left 1966

Aunty Connie and I in Canada 2001

Aunty Connie with Ma and Pa McDuma 1982

Uncle Dan my Mom and me 1952

Uncle John with my sister Joyce Wedding 1988

CHAPTER 6

Verandah

At the time of Moms passing, my sister Dandeleen and I attended a school in Steenberg (Primary No 2). Grandma decided to enroll us at a school closer to her house. She believed that the best school for us would be a Catholic school. Ma believed that these schools provided better education and discipline. She enrolled us at St Anthony's School Bergvliet, which was quite a distance from our house; it was approximately 25 minutes' walk from home. This school was later relocated to a Coloured area because it was situated in an area which would be reserved for Whites only. I started at St Anthony's in Std. 3 (grade 5) in 1963. I was not a favorite with my new teacher. The night before my first day at my new school, Ma washed my hair and cut my bangs. She put a curler in front, so that it could look neat in the morning and I went to bed with a stocking on my head to keep it flat. I had long thick coarse hair, which was not suitable for bangs, but Ma meant well, and I was excited to see the results in the morning.

The next morning, I dressed in my new school uniform and with my new hairstyle, I thought I looked wonderful. After Ma made sure that my hair looked presentable, I set off to my new school, feeling confident and excited at the same time. After checking in at the school office, I was referred to my Std. 3 teacher's classroom. The first thing she said to me in Afrikaans was "waar gaan jy met die afdakkie op jou kop?" (Where are you going with a verandah on your head?). She was referring to my bangs, which were no longer flat and straight, but looked like a verandah shading my forehead. The children in class burst out laughing and I stood there looking like a fool. At that moment, I became very emotional. I was mad at my teacher for turning me into a joke on the very first day and at my Ma for unintentionally making me look like a fool. I was also mad at my Mom for having died and therefore resulting in me having to leave my old school and my friends. I felt as if I was alone in the world with no mother and a group of children laughing at me. That afternoon I went home and did not tell anyone what had happened at school. The next day I brushed my hair back, like I normally did and tied it up with a ribbon. However, for the longest time the children continued to laugh and point to my hair. It made such an impact on the kids, that fifty years later, I met one of my classmates. Although she could not remember my name, she did remember me as the kid who was known as "Afdakkie" (Verandah). I thought wow, fifty years later and that is how I am being remembered, all because of an insensitive teacher. For the rest of the year in that class I hated every bit of it. Luckily, it was only for six months, because I started there in the middle of a school year. My Std. 4 (grade 6) teacher, Miss Kaye, was the opposite. She took a genuine interest in all her students and I always felt special in her class. In fact, she became one of my favorite teachers of all time. I met my best friend in her class, with who I am still in contact with, more than fifty years later. St Anthony's school offered ballet classes, which I took a special interest in and first aid which was beneficial to all. On a Friday morning the school had to attend morning mass at the nearby Catholic Church. Although I was not Catholic, nothing stopped me from attending mass. After mass we would go back to school and get treated to hot chocolate and sandwiches. Every morning before school we would have assembly in the school hall and our Sister Superior, who was the school Principal, would lead the school in prayer and send us to our classrooms. The nuns who were in charge were extremely strict and did believe in corporal punishment. We would be sent to the Principal's office for punishment when needed which would involve a ruler over your knuckles. The school also had a charity to which we donated to every day, called "Holy Childhood". Every week my Uncle Dan would give me 10 cents pocket money which I would budget, 1 cent for the charity every day, and 1 cent for an ice sucker to consume on my way home from school. St Anthony's is where I finished my primary school years Std. 5 (grade 7) and moved on to high school.

CHAPTER 7

High School

After I finished at St Anthony's, Ma enrolled me at Wittebome High School in Wynberg. This used to be an all-White high school known as John Graham High. Due to the group areas act, the school had to relocate to a White area as it was now situated in an area that was declared for Coloured people. Although there was a high school beside our house, Ma thought that this would be a better school for me to attend, because it had a good reputation. To attend Wittebome High School meant long commute for me; I would have to do a 20-minute walk to Heathfield Station from our house, and then travel by train to Wynberg, and then walk for 7 minutes to get to school from there. This did not make sense to me since Heathfield High School was a 2-minute walk from my house. So off I went to my new school in my smart uniform, blue tunic, white shirt, stripe tie, stripe blue and yellow blazer, cheese -cutter hat, white ankle socks and school shoes (walkers). The hat part of the uniform was discontinued soon after my first year.

Ma accompanied me on the first day, because parents had to attend a briefing. Ma had an outgoing personality and could easily start a conversation with anyone. She would often talk to strangers sitting next to her at the station, or on the train. She had a warm and approachable personality; she often greeted and smiled to people passing her on the street. She loved visiting my school and took advantage of the opportunity to socialize and mingle with the teachers and even the Principal. Ma also decided that even though our home language was Afrikaans, I should be place into an English Higher class and take all my subjects in English. Because of this I had to work extra hard to meet my grades. My subjects In Std. 6 (grade 8) were English Higher, Afrikaans Lower, General Science, General Mathematics, Domestic Science, Geography and Latin. Latin was a subject which I did not like but was particularly good at and averaged 90% during my exams. This helped me to increase my overall percentage in class. The following year I dropped Domestic Science and Latin and replaced it with Accountancy, which together with Mathematics were my favorite subjects. We also had Music and R.I. (religious instruction) classes which most of the time was used by the students to catch up with their homework. Because our house was always crowded, it was hard for me to find a quiet spot to study or do homework. Whenever I had to study for my exam, I would wait till the house is completely quiet and work from the kitchen table or bedroom dressing table, till early hours in the morning; therefore, I would go to school tired the next day, through lack of sleep.

In 1966 when I started at this school, Mr. Africa was

the Principal and was commonly referred to as "Affies" by the students. He was strict, stern, well dressed, always wore a hat and hardly ever smiled. Every Monday morning, we would have assembly in the quad with scripture reading, uniform inspection and weekly updates. His scripture reading was from his favorite two verses in the bible and would alternate every week. By the end of my high school years, I knew these verses by heart. Mr. Africa was also our Accountancy teacher in Std. 9 and 10 (grade 11 and 12) and I would always make sure that I do his homework first, in order to avoid detention, if it were not done. He also had a cane in his office and every so often students would be sent to the office to be disciplined. Our schools also arranged inter house sports every year. At that time there were no inter school competition until much later when it was introduced among the Coloured schools only. The inter house sport was for competition in field sport. I never qualified for this, but I was part of the cheerleading group. The students were divided into four groups namely Blue, Red, Green and Yellow House. On sports day, the four houses would meet at William Herbert Sports Field in Wynberg for competition. We had plenty of fun especially if you were part of the winning team. Non contestants would be in the stand cheering and singing as loud as they could. Mr. Blaaws our Physical Fitness teacher would be the one to organize the event. The senior banquet for the Std.10 (grade 12) would be organized by the Std. 9 (grade 11) pupils on the school property. We did not have a school hall, therefore a partition dividing two classrooms would be taken out to serve as a banquet hall. The room would be decorated, and we would have a simple presentation with all the teachers present. There was no such thing as limousines, tuxedos, or fancy ball gowns. Everything was kept simple, but fun and I even got to dance with my favorite teacher, Mr. Peterson, who taught me mathematics in my senior year. We could bring a partner, but most kids showed up alone.

After all those years I can still remember some of those teachers, who left a mark on me. For instance, my Mathematics teacher who was soft spoken and gentle and who's subject was my favorite. I could not wait to get to his class. My Accountancy teacher Mr. Africa who was also the school Principal; I remember him for after he wrote the balance sheet on the black board. He would stand at the back of the classroom, admire his work, and say "A thing of beauty is a joy forever". The other teacher whom I hated but also loved was my Afrikaans teacher. He was also known as "Cuttie" because of his hairstyle centre path, which reminded us of cut loaf bread. He was also known as "Kweeper" because he would whip us with a quince stick picked from his garden. When he was in a bad mood, he would whip the whole class just to get our attention for no reason. But, when he was in a good mood, he would tell us jokes and have the class in stitches. Sadly, back then teachers would get away with this type of punishment and nobody ever complained. Now that I am thinking of this, I realize how bad it was and that should never have been allowed. Another memorable teacher was my English teacher Miss Corden-Lloyd. She was the only White teacher at our school who was also close to retirement age. She would always accuse me of smoking and no matter how much I told her that I did not smoke she would insist that I did. One day I stayed after class and asked her why she believed that I smoked. She replied that whenever she marked my books she would cough and the reason for her coughing was because she was allergic to smoke. Turns out, that I lived in a house where it was normal for people to smoke inside, with the result, my books were reeking of smoke. After she realized that it was something, I had no control of, she never mentioned it again.

WitteBome High School 1967 Una Dirkse

CHAPTER 8

Spotty Dog

Growing up there was no T.V. in South Africa. The country only introduced this in the mid-seventies. Prior to this we were into sports on Saturdays. In my case I played hockey for a team called Wynberg Swifts. My Aunt Connie and I played for the same team. She played center forward, whereas I played center half. Our team was in the third division and not considered good, but we had a blast every Saturday afternoon, having fun on the field. Those years the sports facilities for Coloured people were in poor shape, for instance, there were no toilets on the field and no change rooms or showers. Whenever we needed to use a toilet, we had to run to the nearest house and ask for permission to use their facility. Apart from sports on a Saturday, we had a Bioscope in Retreat Road (Princess Bioscope) approximately ten minutes' walk from our house. Living in a community where everyone was known to one another, this was a special meeting place for kids at the 12 noon show of the bioscope. My sister Dandeleen and I would get 25 cents each for the movie and 10 cents each for a bag of chips at interval. During the movie, the kids did not pay much attention. They would fool around with their friends, throw popcorn at one another and run up and down the aisles. I think the parents used to send their kids to the cinema to have some quiet time. The cinema also had a 4 p.m. show for the teens, which was more reserved and a show at 8 p.m. for the adults. I remember watching my uncles dressed in suit and tie and my aunts also dressed up to see a movie, unlike today where people are dressed more casually to watch movies (ex. dressed in shorts and flip flops). The Princess Bioscope played an important role in our area because this was the only cinema for Coloured people, which were within walking distance. Apart from movies, the cinema also hosted celebrities like Percy Sledge and many other well-known artists. Next to the cinema was a hotel which was also owned by the same cinema owners, which was Quibell Brothers. Later Quibell Brothers built a second theatre for Coloureds, known as the Luxurama Theatre in Wittebome, which became the hot spot for entertainment.

Later when Dandeleen and I became older, Ma would allow us to attend the 4 p.m. shows. She also gave us permission to see Percy Sledge live in concert and after the show we stood in a line-up to get his autograph. Ma was strict when it came to socializing and having given us permission to see our first live concert, with our friends, was a big deal for us. For the longest time I would try to dance like Percy Sledge and just wear bell bottoms like he did. I became his biggest fan. My Aunt Connie was an usher at the Bioscope, therefore complimentary tickets were always available for certain shows for us.

My Uncle John who was Ma's second eldest son, owned a Chevrolet Opel, either late forties, or early fifties model. At the time he was the only one on our street, who owned a motor vehicle and now and again he would drive Ma and us to Kalk Bay beach. This beach was the only beach for Coloured people which were accessible by train. All the beaches along the railway line were for Whites only. Sad as it may sound, on a hot day, Kalk Bay beach would be so crowded that there was hardly space to walk. Ma would pack a pot of food for our lunch and a primus stove on which to heat it. She would also make a tin of cream crackers and cheese and fruit mainly consisting of oranges and apples and if she had extra money, she would buy us ice cream. Our journey to the beach would take us down main road Tokai and as kids we would use "Spotty Dog" restaurant as a landmark. This building was canine shaped and painted white with black spots. It was situated in Lakeside between Muizenberg and Wynberg. Later a kennel was added to the dog's tail to create more space for the restaurant. It was a place for hamburgers and ice cream, but at the time was only open to White people. In 1970 Spotty Dog was involved in a road accident, when a truck rammed into it. A replica of the dog remains today, on the same spot. Once we reached Spotty Dog, we would get excited knowing that we are getting closer to the beach. Kalk Bay was also and still is a fishing village with a harbour. That time the fishermen used their boats to make extra money and sell a trip around the bay for a tiekie (three pennies) which were also part of the fun. The kids would take a ride for "tiekie" around the bay with no life jackets. At other times we would travel by train, which meant that we had to leave by 6 a.m. in order to get a spot on the beach under the tunnels in the shade. After a fun filled day, Ma would take us back on the train with sandy bushy hair and almost all the time we would fall asleep on the train ride home which lasted about fifteen minutes. A day at the beach was always fun for a child and still is.

CHAPTER 9

Sisters

I was the eldest, my sister Dandeleen was the second eldest, Janet (Jeanette) third, Daphne forth and our baby sister Joyce. Ma decided to name Joyce after our mother who had the same name. Being so soon after Mom's passing, nobody wanted to call her by that name, and everybody just referred to her as "Baby". She was known as Baby by everyone in the area, except school and later work. Many years later when Joyce was an adult and our kids started calling her "Aunty Baby" she asked everyone to call her by her name. My sister Daphne had a twin, but sadly our brother died at birth. Dad was heartbroken at losing what would have been his only son and always made mention of it. Growing up Ma would always remind me that because I was the eldest, I should be an example to my siblings and take care of Joyce the youngest. By this time, I was old enough to see that Joyce gets bathed at night and that her hair was brushed and ready for bed. When Joyce started grade 1, Ma decided to send her to St Anthony's like the rest of us. From the very start Joyce hated school and being spoiled by Ma, she would throw a tantrum every morning, knowing that she might get to stay home, and it almost always worked. Because Ma was illiterate, I was the one who would have to write the letter to the teacher, explaining why Joyce could not make it for school. I remember my letter to the teacher was always in the same wording and reason. I would even sign Ma's name. One day I told Ma that she cannot keep making excuses for Joyce not being at school. Ma told me that, in that case, as from then, it would be my responsibility to see that Joyce gets to school in the morning. I suddenly realized that it would have been better for me to have kept quiet. From that day onwards, it was a different procedure for me in the morning. I would have to get up extra early, prepare myself for school and then see to Joyce. When ready for school, Joyce would start sniffing, coughing and then crying all to get Ma's attention. Sometimes she would hide which meant I had to spend extra time to find her. Walking Joyce to school meant that I had to walk from home to St Anthony's in Bergvliet, make sure that she is in her classroom in case she runs home and then walk back to Heathfield station in time for my train to Wynberg. The timing for me in the morning was especially important, because should I miss my train, it meant that I would be late for school and therefore detention after school. On a good day Joyce would be crying all the way to school and on a bad day she would sit on the pavement. I would then have to pull her by the hand, hold her school case and carry my school satchel. Those years the kids did not carry back packs. We either had a school case or when in high school we would carry a satchel. Later when Joyce became used to her school and made friends, she was happy to walk with the other kids, although I still had to make sure that she was properly dressed for school. Ma had a coal stove in her kitchen which meant that she had to light a fire in order to make us porridge before we went to school. All this was a normal everyday way of life, yet with all the convenience of today, we still find things to complain about. Although Joyce became more independent, as she grew older, I always thought that it was my responsibility to look out for her. Later when I started working, I would buy her toiletries every month and give her money whenever she needed it.

My sisters and I were awfully close. We had a bond and still have. Growing up we had our differences, but it would be over in no time. As a teen, my sister Dandeleen and I would hang out with the same friends and as a result we were more like friends than sisters. Ma, although strict always wanted to know who our friends were and never stopped us from bringing our friends home. If she felt that we were hanging out with the wrong crowd, she would quickly let us know and she was always right. I guess parents knew when to step in.

Growing up we all had thick long coarse hair. We became more aware of our appearance and our hair became the focus. Our middle sister Janet decided that she should be the one to be our hairdresser. She was also the one who would get us all into trouble with Ma. That time there were no fancy hair grooming equipments and Janet's method of hair straightening was simple and ancient. We would wait until Ma go to bed and quietly proceed to the kitchen to straighten our hair. This method would involve placing an old blanket on the kitchen table. We would then place our head on the blanket, brush our hair out and then place brown paper over our hair and use the clothing iron to iron it straight. Almost like ironing wrinkles out of a shirt. If Janet were not satisfied with the result, she would rub Vaseline on our hair to make it smooth. After that, our hair would be straight but also stiff. One night, Janet did Daphne's hair and accidently burnt Daphne's ears. Daphne went screaming, Ma woke up and that was the last of Janet's hairdressing career. Later, when "Wellastrate" became the popular hair relaxer, we were old enough to chemically straighten one another's hair and that solved our hair problems. My Dad later bought me a hooded hairdryer for my birthday, which became family property.

Living in a house with our Aunts Veronica, Connie and Sarah and our Uncles Dan and John, we always had music in our house. Uncle Dan was a huge jazz fanatic. Ma allowed him to turn his bedroom into a "jazz workshop" as he called it. Every weekend he would have his friends over for a get together. They would play their music which we became accustomed to. My Aunt Connie shared a room with myself, Dandeleen, Janet and Daphne. When Mom died Daphne was only three years old. Aunt Connie was twenty at the time and decided to care for Daphne as if she was her own. Daphne in turn believed that Aunt Connie was her Mom, until later when it was made clear to her, that our mom had died when she was young, and that Aunt Connie stepped in and cared for her. Joyce always shared Ma's bedroom. In our bedroom we had a record player and tape recorder on the dressing table. Aunt Connie loved to listen to Andy Williams, Cliff Richards, Tom Jones, Connie Frances, Dusty Springfield; all these artists were popular at the time. There was also a famous South African group called "The Flames" who originated from Durban. Their hit song, "For your precious love" was Aunt Connie's favorite. At that time in order to catch the lyrics to the song one would have to play the song repeatedly. Aunt Connie would sit with pen and paper and try to catch the lyrics, while we as children had to endure all this. This song was also covered by Otis Redding. Sometimes we would have fun by singing these songs and record ourselves. At other times we would play board games like Snakes and Ladders, or Monopoly. Apart from this as I mentioned before Aunt Sarah played the piano and not forgetting Uncle John and his piano accordion, there were always a sense of happiness in our house and although poor we always felt rich and loved. On Friday nights we would listen to the hit parade on the radio and count down to the number 1 hit for the week. Saturday nights, when our aunts go out, it would be our turn to apply makeup, and dress in their clothing and high heel shoes. As kids we never had many toys because I assumed there were no money for this. I always dreamt of having a bicycle, but this never materialized. As kids, it was common for us to run barefoot to the Bhai shop (Indian convenience store) to get candy. For 1 cent we could get three candies. The smell in the Bhai shop had a mixture of fruits, sweets, spices and incense sticks which would burn in the store. The radio played an important part in growing up. A pop song would come up and we would all burst out in song. Aunt Connie would come home from work; bury candies under our pillow which we had to save for bedtime. Unconditional love overflowed our home all the time.

Growing up, my Aunt Sarah paid special attention to me knowing that I was at the age when I was conscious of my appearance. She would design my dresses before Ma takes the fabric to the dressmaker. She had a flare for design and would always sketch her own style of clothes before heading out with her fabrics. Many times, she would take me to her hairdresser, who would straighten my hair with a hot comb which was common at the time. I would leave the salon with straight sleek hair, until the rain or mist takes it back to its original form. Apart from that I would be the one to accompany her to choir practice and as I mentioned she used to be the organist at church. Later when Dandeleen and I grew older, Ma would not let us out without an adult; Aunt Sarah would step in, drop us off and pick us up. Aunt Sarah was a ballroom dancer, because of this she took a keen interest in my ballet dancing. She always tried to teach me to ballroom dance and would move the kitchen table to provide space. Our bedroom had an inter-leading door to the kitchen and Aunt Sarah would teach me by utilizing the kitchen and the bedroom as a dance floor. At other times she would play the piano and get me to show my ballet moves.

Aunt Connie played an important role in our lives. I remember at night after we prepared for bed, we could not wait to see what she buried under the pillow which we could only eat when in bed. It could be a candy, chocolate or cookie, but there would always be something. Sometimes after being out with her friends, she would come home late at night, wake us up and treat us to fries and chicken bought from the local take-out. She would come in the bedroom and say "hey guys look what I got"; although half asleep, we would sit up and munch on fries and chicken. As a special treat she would take us to Cape Town once a month by train. Our first stop would be to Cape Town gardens, where we would feed the squirrels and later walk us to the only restaurant in Cape Town for Coloureds known as the "La Fiesta". Here we would wait in a line-up for a seat inside. Once inside, she would buy us each a banana split, which was simply made up of banana, chocolate, ice-cream and fresh cream if I remember well. After that we would visit the parade where one could get anything from a "needle to an anchor". She basically went there, to look through the used records to see if anything interested her. Our last stop would be to her friend, who worked at Nannuci dry cleaners on the parade, which also became a place for friends to meet and hang-out on a Saturday after shopping. After that we would make our way back to the station but not before stopping for a meat pie sold on the parade. I should also mention that while sitting on the train and waiting for it to depart, there would be the ice-cream vendor cycling up and down the station hoping to sell to riders. By this time Aunt Connie would be broke and would ignore the vendor. This was simple true love that we as kids got to enjoy.

While Aunt Sarah paid special attention to me and Aunt Connie to Daphne, Aunt Veronica focused her attention on Dandeleen and Janet, while Ma cared for Joyce. Aunt

Veronica, Ma's youngest daughter was only eighteen when mom passed away. Being at an age when she was ready to hang out with her friends and party, she had no choice but to put that aside and help Ma care for us. When I started menstruating at age 11, it was Aunt Veronica in whom I consulted and who guided me. That time adults did not sit down with their children and explained what is happening to their bodies during this time, therefore Ma would never touch on that subject. Having had such a wonderful caring family, we were the luckiest motherless children. There were lots of kids like us, who were either abandoned, or placed in foster homes or orphanages.

Although my Uncle John (Gawie) annoyed me with his singing and playing of the piano accordion, I was never afraid to ask him for a ride in his Chevy to my school meetings, or hockey games. Uncle Dan on the other hand would give me pocket money without me having to ask. Daphne was also Uncle Dan's favorite. He nicknamed her "Bugsie" as in Bugs Bunny because of her love of raw carrots. She would always be nibbling on a carrot whenever Ma prepared it for cooking. My mother loved her brothers very dearly and whenever they came to visit us in Banjo Street, Mom would make them a special treat which they loved. She would fry frikkadels (hamburgers) and they swore that their sister, my mother, was the Queen when it came to cooking frikkadels.

From an early age, Mom used to teach Dandeleen and I, how to knit and sew. We started off by sewing and knitting for our dolls. We each had one doll and mine was called "Annie". At night, mom would remind us to put our dolls in pajamas, which we sewed and place them on the couch for the night. Growing up, Dandeleen and I, knew how to knit our own scarves and hats and even altered our clothes by using Ma's sewing machine, which we would either place on the kitchen table or on the dressing table in our bedroom.

Growing up at that time, everything was segregated. Even as a child one had to read the signs which was common, either "Whites Only" or "Non-Whites Only" signs all over the place. Separate benches on the train station, separate couches on the trains, separate post office entrances, and separate ticket booking offices on the train stations. Some stations had separate bridges for pedestrians to cross. There was a particular incidence when Dandeleen and I went to church one Sunday morning. Our church St Cyprians used to be at Retreat Station on the opposite side of the railway line. In order to get there, we had to walk pass the "Whites Only" bridge to cross at the non-white bridge then walk back to get to church, thereby adding an extra five minutes to our commute. On this Sunday, we were running late for church and thought we would take a chance and used the Whites-Only bridge therefore cutting down on time. To our dismay, when we got to the other side, there was a white police officer greeting us. He gave us strict instructions never to use the bridge or anything marked Whites-Only and chased us back to cross at the other bridge assigned for Non-Whites. As kids we were terrified that day; we got to church late, shaky and upset. Later when we grew older, we were confirmed in St Cyprians Church and served as Sunday School teachers. Whenever I spoke to Pa about the humiliation of Apartheid, he would always remind me that skin colour means nothing and that I should think of myself as equal to my White skin citizens. These values I learned from Ma and Pa McDuma and growing up I saw myself as equal despite Apartheid.

My husband Joey, my sister Joyce, Daphne, me in the center, Aunty Veronica, Janet and Dandeline 2012

CHAPTER 10

Tralee Road

We lived at Tralee Road Heathfield, which at the time was a dirt road with twenty neatly built cottages; ten on each side of the road facing each other. On Consort Road which ran parallel to Tralee Road, there were five more of these cottages all neatly built with wood and iron. At the time, all the properties belonged to Mr. Punt, who also owned a farm running adjacent to Tralee Road and Consort Road. The area was then known as Punts Cottages. When we moved to Ma's house, she had already reared most of her children there. The original house had two bedrooms, a kitchen with coal stove, and a living room. There were no indoor toilets, therefore we used an outhouse which was replaced once a week with a clean drum. Although these were rental cottages, Ma would expand her house as her family grew larger. By the time we moved to Ma she had five bedrooms, three of which were added on. Later the property and farm went up for auction and Mr. Willemse bought all the cottages which he later sold giving the tenants first option to buy. Most of the tenants opted not to but Ma was smart and bought her house for 7000 Rand (fifty years ago). Ma and Pa started to renovate their property and rebuilt with brick according to government standards. While Tralee Road was owned by Mr. Punt, it had no drainage or plumbing. The old sand road would turn into a slippery, muddy mess after it had rained. The kids would have fun sliding, throwing, and building sandcastles with the muddy sand; kids got creative and would replicate boats and mountains with the mud. I was too big for this type of fun, but my sisters Joyce, Daphne, and Janet had a blast during this time. I hated having to jump over puddles whenever I got home from school, after it had rained.

Tralee Road was a community where the adults looked out for one another's children. It was normal for adults in the community to discipline or report to the other parents when their kids stepped out of line. As kids we knew exactly who would be the first to report to Ma should we misbehave. When we saw Mrs. Brown sitting on Ma's porch, we knew we were in trouble. Mrs. Brown was also known as "Loeloe" to Ma and everyone else in the community. She was also known to gather gossip and spread it around the neighbourhood. After she came to Ma with a bit of gossip, she would at the same time ask to borrow a cup of sugar or a cup of rice. Ma would often remind her to return whatever she borrowed. Sometimes, before she starts her gossips, Ma would ask her what it is that she needed first, in exchange for her story. Mrs. Brown also had a big family and struggled to make ends meet. Because the residents knew our mother and knew what extra responsibilities Ma had taken on, they all played a part in our well-being. Ma would buy cheaper fabric from "Ackerman's Store" in Wynberg and give it to the dressmaker across the road, who would stitch our dresses for free.

Once a year, my Uncle Dan's friend, William Adams, commonly known as "Boy" would donate our new church hats for Christmas. He worked at a hat factory and at the end of the year, before the factory closed for vacation, Boy would check with Ma to see what colour hats she preferred for us. Almost all the time, she would choose white hats to match our Sunday clothes. The Chinese Variety Store on Retreat Road known as Lings Store, where Ma was a loyal customer, would donate our socks and underwear and white gloves for church. That time the kids would attend church or Sunday school dressed in hats, bags, gloves, and bobby socks. I guess what I am trying to say is that the whole community helped Ma to provide for her grandkids. This is the outpouring of love which we never talk about but is there all the time.

Ma had wonderful neighbours. On one side lived Mrs. Segers, who adopted me as her hairdresser. Every so often she would call me to cut her hair. Even when offered, I would never accept payment, but after I did her hair, she would make me sit at the table and give me a bowl of soup. I swear she made the best soup, and I can still picture the dumplings and marrow bones in the soup, together with the taste of parsley, carrots, and peas. On the other side of Ma's house lived Mrs. Adams, who was blind with a big family and who's daughters were my friends. Between our house and Mrs. Adams was a high corrugated fence which divided the properties. On a Monday, Ma and Mrs. Adams would do their laundry by hand. Ma would do our laundry on our side of the fence and Mrs. Adams would do hers on her side of the fence. Although they could not see one another, because of the height of the fence, they would have a conversation going. Now and then, Mrs. Adams would call me to run over and check whether she washed the shirt collars clean. I was always amazed at how she navigated around her house with her disability (blindness), when doing her chores or even cooking. The residence in Tralee Road would call each other by their last name. Ma would call "Adams" and she would reply "Mc Duma ", and they would start chatting. The conversation would always be about the "change of life". One day I asked Ma what it meant, and she told me that it was adult conversation and that I should not listen in. Much later, I learned that it meant menopause but that time it was called "change of life". Almost all the residence had a fruit tree. Mrs. Adams had a quince tree, Mrs. Segers had a mulberry tree, and Ma had a grape vine and a guava tree. Fresh fruit would be shared back and forth.

When the Group Areas Act took place all the Black people who lived on our street had to relocate to areas allocated for Blacks as our area was now classified as a Coloured area. Some of the kids that had to move were my friends and even as kids we were aware of the cruelty of Apartheid. The Group Areas Act uprooted many communities and caused a lot of heartache for many families. After the property were sold, only a small number of tenants bought. Many moved out to other Coloured areas such as Steenberg, Lavender

Hill, and Mitchells Plain. New owners moved in and over the years Tralee Road became an upgraded neighborhood; they installed new tar road, drainage, streetlights, and fancy well-built brick homes. The old Tralee Road will always have a special place in my heart because this is where my childhood memories were made.

I remember there would always be somebody having tea on our porch. Many times, when we came from school, the neighbours would be on our step (porch) listening to a 4 p.m. radio talk show called "So Maak Mens" (This is how you do it); it was hosted by Esme Everad and Jan Cronje. This show dealt with news, methods, stories, knitting and a recipe at the end. After the show, Ma would say something to the affect that, those recipes are old and outdated and that the show should do better than that. Ma was an exceptionally good cook, and Pa was a qualified chef therefore, between the two we ate well. Sometimes, Ma did not want Pa to cook because she thought he was too extravagant. We also had bad element that would stand around on our street corner. They did not live on our street but chose a corner as a meeting place. Although they never harmed or molested anyone, they would stand and sing on the corner which was annoying. One time I heard a baby crying in their midst. I went to look, and found a baby approximately six months old, in wet diapers in the arms of a drunken mother. This upset me terribly. I asked the mother if I could take the baby home for a bath, food, and a change of clothing. She agreed to come with me. After I bathed and dressed the baby in my cousins clothing (who was about the same age), I fed and gave the mom a fresh bottle of milk for the infant. While I was doing this, Ma paid special attention and asked the mother to bring the baby every day for something to eat. Ma tried to find out where she lived and how she could care for an infant while under the influence of liquor. She did not want to share any information, and we assumed that she was homeless. The next day I went looking for the mom and baby where I found them the previous day, but they were nowhere to be found. For the longest time I could not get this baby out of my mind, and always wondered if the baby ever survived. There were many homeless families in our area. Further along, there were shanties that provided shelter for many homeless people, but I always felt that the government should have provided more for families with children. Luckily at the time, we did not have to pay for education. Some schools even offered food to their students.

Ma and Pa were well known in Tralee Road, and the surrounding areas of Heathfield and Retreat. Ma had an outgoing personality, which people gravitated to. She was about 5ft 8" and had a slender built. She was upright and whenever she went out, she would be impeccably dressed and as I mentioned before she had no problem starting a conversation with a stranger. Pa on the other hand, did not have the same outgoing qualities as Ma, but when Pa spoke, he would be worthwhile listening to, because you could always learn something. Like Ma, Pa was also very smart in the way that he dressed and although Pa was very well educated and Ma was not, they made a remarkably good team.

In Tralee Road the residence would address each other

by their last name i.e., Ma and Pa were known as Mr. and Mrs. McDuma. All the kids on the street showed tremendous respect towards the residence and in return the residence looked out for one another's children. We would not dare step out of line, because somebody would report to your parents. Some of the residence on the road had a landline and one resident even had a dishwasher. We did not have this but my Uncle John who was commonly known as "Gawie" in the area, did own a car which was a rare commodity at the time. When Uncle John (Gawie) drove his brown Chevy down the road, I swear he thought he was the mayor in the street. That Chevy was his pride and joy and was also used to attract girls. Many years later when I had already started to work, we obtained a landline. I would envy my friends who had a telephone at home and thought they were rich. When we had to make a call, we would go to the Bhai shop (Indian grocery store) who charged us, or we would use the public booth called "tiekie box" at the time. Some kids knew how to manipulate the wires at the tiekie box, in order to make a free call. There were not a lot of facilities for Coloured people. The residence or the local church would come up with creative ideas to keep the kids occupied. They would organize a movie in the local church hall with an overhead projector, which would break down at the crucial part of the movie. At this point, the kids would become noisy until the problem is solved, and the show can go on. A lot of the time the parents insisted that the movie have a biblical theme. Other parents would organize a "curry and rice" event which was music, dance and at the end of the evening a meal of curry and rice.

My favourite event would be a "mystery drive", where we would get on a rented bus and get driven to a venue where we could braai (BBQ). The venue would be the mystery.

Tralee Road was also known to have a shebeen (illegal house selling liquor) on the corner. My uncles, especially Uncle Arthur who was commonly known as "Karols" or "Rolsie" as Ma would call him was a frequent visitor to the shebeen. Uncle Arthur was considered a boarder and had a room in the backyard. It is said that he was Ma's biological child and our biological uncle. Ma had him when she was young, and her sister raised Uncle Arthur as their own. Uncle Arthur knew that Ma was his biological mother, but she never acknowledged it. Sadly, Ma passed away without doing so. In those days 1920's I guess it would have been a scandal to have a child out of wedlock, therefore it would have been kept a secret in the family. Whenever Uncle Arthur would refer to Ma as his mother, she would turn the hose pipe on him to shut him up. He would then retreat into his room and keep quiet. One day he grabbed the hose pipe from her and turned it onto her. She stood in the backyard drenched. For the children it was funny and left us giggling little to say that Ma was not amused. Uncle Arthur had an account at the shebeen and on a Friday when he got paid, he would first pay the shebeen owner and send me to pay his cigarette account at the Bhai shop, and off course I would get money for a chocolate. Ma was very motherly towards Uncle Arthur. As I said she affectionately called him "Rolsie" and made sure that his room was clean and that he always had clean clothes and beddings. The family knew about the relationship between the two, but this would never come up in a conversation with Ma present. He was a few years older than my mother and would often remind me that he was our biological uncle. During the 2nd world war, he signed up and was enlisted to drive a truck and pick-up deceased bodies. Non-White soldiers were used to doing mediocre jobs like stretcher bearers and truck drivers. Over the years I think he was still traumatized by this. Whenever he was intoxicated, he would mention this and talk about how at the end of the war, as compensation, the Non-Whites were given bicycles and the Whites were given cars. I never verified this, but he did have an old bicycle which he never used. This almost always, put him in a bad mood and would cause him to leave the conversation. Later in life Uncle Arthur lost a leg due to complications of diabetes. This did not stop him from going to the shebeen in his wheelchair. Everyone on Tralee Road knew about him and his bad habits, but he was a part of the community and was tolerated. One night he was so drunk that he passed out on the street. Our family dog named Billie came to fetch Pa at home and led him to where Uncle Arthur was. So yes, even the dog looked out for him. Now Uncle Arthur had a friend who lived across the road by the name of Mr. Jackson who was also his shebeen buddy. The two would share liquor and when tipsy would start arguing. A lame boxing match would develop; both missing each other's punches because they are so drunk. Ma would get in between, chase Uncle Arthur to his room like a child, and ban Mr. Jackson from our house. Ma paid particular attention to Mrs. Jackson. Every so often, she would run over to their house with soup. While she is there, she would remind Mr. Jackson that he is banned from our house. The banning order only lasted until next time he shared a drink with Uncle Arthur and the same lame boxing match would occur. Ma was fearless; she spoke her mind and gained respect from others naturally.

Mrs. Jackson would buy fish on credit from the fish monger, borrow money from Ma to buy fish oil in which to fry her fish, and later borrow a cup of rice to cook with her fish. Borrowing a cup of rice, sugar, milk, or other food essentials was common in our street. Vegetables would be bought from the vegetable vendor who was known to everyone as "Maan", who made good business on Tralee Road. On Fridays he would sell his fresh vegetables and collect payment for the previous weeks produce which he sold on credit. His customers would always have a running tab. Maan's last stop would be Ma's house. This is where he gets a cup of coffee or soup and chat with Ma. While he was chatting, the kids in the street would take and munch on his fruits. I think Maan knew they were doing this, but he pretended not to notice. I am not sure whether Mrs. Jackson ever returned or repaid whatever she borrowed from Ma, but Ma had this soft spot for her. My grandma was phenomenal, she shared whatever she could and would often get little in return. Mrs. Jackson had her daughter and ten grandchildren living with her. My Aunt Connie sold fresh chicken and eggs for a local businessman, who paid her commission on whatever she sold. On Fridays he would drop it off and once again Mrs. Jackson was her loyal customer. She would buy the chicken and eggs and pay the following Friday for the current order. She was always in debt with Aunty Connie, who like Ma, would give whatever they could and not expect anything in return. Late payments for chicken and eggs were common in Tralee Road. I am not even sure whether Aunty Connie ever got paid her expected commission. All the children on the street loved Aunty Connie. When they saw her walking down the street they would run and chant her name.

Christmas in Tralee Road was amazing. There were no fancy gifts, except for a pair of new pajamas that would be wrapped under the tree for each child. Our focus would be the giant turkey that would be prepared by Pa who was a qualified chef. I remember Pa's stuffing which I could not get enough of. Besides turkey, Ma would do roast beef with vegetable and gravy. That was the only time of the year, that we would see so much meat. As kids we would first eat our rice and vegetables and save our meat for last. The Christmas preparation would start a few days before. Dad would come and paint the kitchen and living room, while the owner at the Variety Store would come and lay new linoleum on the kitchen floor. Ma would order a huge cake from the bakery, while Pa would start his homemade ginger beer. The ginger beer was a special treat from Pa, which only happened at Christmas time. It was brewed in a huge container before the time and Christmas lunch would never be the same without Pa's homemade ginger beer. Ma would make her Christmas steam pudding. She would bury a silver coin inside and get the children excited to see who would be the lucky one to find it. On Christmas Eve the children got to decorate the tree and lay out their new clothes for the morning church service. We would be dressed in everything new, but all donated from friends and community. I almost forgot to mention, the Christmas band/choir that would be walking down Tralee Road at midnight playing carols. The community would be outside and some of the adults would follow the band on their route. Besides our big family, Ma would also invite Aunty Annie with her six grandchildren, Aunty Patricia (who was an ex-girlfriend of Uncle Arthurs), and her cousin Aunty Hannah, who had no other living relative besides Ma. Yes, Ma had plenty of love and plenty of food for everyone.

My Mom Joyce Anthony Tralee Rd 1951

Tralley Rd Me and Ma between 1967 and 1971

CHAPTER 11

Work

While at school (grade 11 &12), I was fortunate to have a part-time job, because back then, it was hard to find student jobs, especially if you were non-white. In my case, I was given the opportunity by my Uncle Dan, who worked at a furniture factory in Houtbay. Uncle Dan was a qualified carpenter; he also managed the factory. He asked his employer if I could come after school on Thursdays, to do the staff wages, so they can be ready for Friday pay-outs. His employer agreed to hire me; they also provided training in that field. The factory was small and only had about ten employees in total. After school every Thursday, I would take a bus from Wynberg Station to Houtbay. When I get there, I would do the wages and whatever other administrative tasks required from me at work. I got paid 10 Rand, of which I would come home and give Ma half and used the rest for odds and ends as I needed. At this time during Apartheid, jobs were advertised in the newspaper in fine print at the bottom of the advertisement page. The paper would read "We regret Whites-only" or "Only White persons need apply". This was humiliating; as a result, I would read the fine print first. After I graduated from high school, I was not inclined to study further and started to look for full-time employment. My first full-time job was at a popular ladies clothing chain store in Cape Town. Here I was employed as a Salesperson. Having to comply by the government regulations and although I was the only Coloured employee, they had to provide separate lunchroom facilities for me. At first, I mingled freely among my colleagues in the same lunchroom but was later told by the "tea lady" that a single table, with one chair, situated at the end of the room, was allocated for me. I felt terribly humiliated and decided not to use the lunchroom at all. Apart from this, I was not happy at this store and resigned after three months. Back then, companies would hire a "tea lady" whose main function was to serve tea to the staff and run errands as needed. My next job was at a high-end clothing store also in Cape Town, who catered to tourist. At this store the pay was better and the facilities were separate, but comfortable. They employed quite a few Coloured people. While working here, I continued to look for better employment. When I heard that the banks were hiring Coloured staff, I submitted my application immediately. Prior to this, the banks only hired "White persons". I applied at a popular Bank on Plein Street, Cape Town, which were the banks central depot. After a few interviews, I was hired by the bank. Here I was employed to work in the cheque processing department and was required to operate a proof machine, used to sort cheques drawn on other banks. This would involve punching in bank identification numbers with one hand and with the other hand, pick up cheques one at a time from a stack; punch in the amount of the cheques and place it in the appropriate slot. The machine sorted the cheques into pockets for eventual return to the bank, on which it was drawn, with a record of activity on a paper tape. At the time when I joined the bank, it was still largely un-automated. A skillful operator was expected to process about 1000 cheques per hour. Once we achieved that amount, we would qualify for an extra bonus. In those days, bank staff wore smart uniforms. While the males wore suit and tie, the ladies wore dresses with matching jackets. When I joined the bank, the white staff wore navy blue dresses and jackets, while the non-white staff wore mustard or "canary yellow" jackets and dresses. Later the bank decided to provide the same uniforms for all staff. Here again we were paid less than the Whites and was told never to discuss our salary with anyone. In the bank everyone was referred to by their last name. In my case I was known as "Miss Anthony" which was my maiden name. After working at the clearing centre for about two years, I was transferred to the banks Woodstock branch. I saw this, as an opportunity to advance, but chances were slim. Here I was employed in Data Capture and once again, I was the only Coloured employee. This branch made a separate lunchroom and toilet for me, according to government regulations. Later they employed another Coloured girl and while our White colleagues shared a tiny lunchroom, we enjoyed our own, where we could relax and snooze during our lunch hour, to our advantage. I later asked for a transfer to the bank's branch in Muizenberg, which was closer to my home. This branch was on Main Road Muizenberg, which was about a five-minute walk to the beach, which was allocated to "Whites-only". By this time, the banks had done away with separate amenities for White and Non-white staff and we were free to use one common lunchroom and toilet.

Thinking back, one of my friends who worked at another bank that was situated in a shopping mall, was not allowed to use the facilities in the branch; she was asked to use the public toilet in the mall. This was at first, when banks started workplace diversity. There was one year at my branch in Muizenberg, where the Manager arranged a Christmas party for the staff, at a nearby hotel open to "Whites-only". He called me into his office to inform and apologize for the fact that I would not be able to attend the work Christmas party. He told me that although I was not invited to attend, he would still ask for special permission from the management team for me to attend. I thanked him, but also told him that I refused to go, where special permission had to be obtained as I was not a criminal. Although, he did get a permit for me at the end, I did not attend the party. The following year, he arranged a party at his home. This way, everyone could enjoy it. I worked at this bank for ten years and later joined two other financial institutions.

Over the years in my experience with South African financial institutions 1971-1988, a lot of changes took place. They hired more "Coloured" staff, and later when they branched out into "Coloured" areas, the staff were given supervisory and management opportunities. Back then, all male Tellers carried firearms in full view of the customers and all banks provided bullet proof glass for safety to the employers. Most banks also operated agencies, in certain areas. My branch in Muizenberg operated an agency in Mitchells Plain, which was a newly developed area for "Coloureds". Every morning three tellers would be transported in an armored vehicle, with cash to operate at the agency. One Monday morning, one of our Teller, during the day, took his firearm to the men's toilet facility and used it to commit suicide. Nobody could understand why he did this, as he celebrated his engagement to his girlfriend on the Saturday prior to the incident. We also had an agency at Blue Route Mall in Tokai, where I served as a Teller and got to be a Savings Bank Supervisor and worked in the Ledger Department. The bank paid a good salary with pension and medical benefits, not forgetting that the salaries were still not equal, to that of our "White" colleagues. After working at this bank for ten years, I resigned to take care of my two sons, Justin aged 6 and Ryan aged 2 at the time. Later, I accepted job offers at other financial institutions.

While living in Ma's house, I was required to bring my pay home untouched. She would then give me pocket money for the month and pay my travelling expenses and my clothing account. I did not like this arrangement and later asked her, whether I could pay for board and lodging instead. This did not go well with Ma and Pa and after a long discussion, they decided on a fixed amount for me to pay. Ma's argument was that, after all the years, she sacrificed for us, it was only right, that she should be compensated in this way. Pa agreed with Ma and for a long time, I was not a favourite. I was not extravagant with money and felt that, had I not done it that way, I would never have been able to save for my wedding reception or even a wedding dress. Later when my sisters left school and started to work, they had to bring their pay home untouched and Ma would pay them pocket money, travelling expenses and their clothing account.

During my time at the banks, the institution would close for business at 1 p.m. on a Wednesday, and at 11 a.m. on a Saturday. This gave me ample time to play my hockey game on a Saturday afternoon, and continue my part-time job at the furniture factory on a Wednesday afternoon. This time, I negotiated, for more pay. During this period in South Africa, the stores would close at 1 p.m. on a Saturday and re-open on a Monday morning. This was a perfect time for families to spend time together, unlike today, when we all seem to be rushing around every day of the week. When I first joined the Bank in 1971, my starting salary was R125.00 per month which was considered good pay at the time. I paid Ma and Pa R80.00 per month for my board and lodging, as we decided, and was left with enough money to save for travel as I always wanted to be able to travel.

In 1972 my friend and I decided to embark on a three-week bus tour from Cape Town to Rhodesia, later known as Zimbabwe and Lorenzo Marques, later known as Maputo. These two destinations were popular among tourists at the time. We started our trip from Cape Town to Port Elizabeth, East London, Durban, Swaziland, Maputo and

Zimbabwe. Our trip included hotel accommodation and two meals per day, either breakfast and dinner or breakfast and lunch. On our return to Cape Town, we passed through a different route touching on at Pretoria and Kimberly. This was my first travel experience and after that nothing could stop me from fulfilling my dreams. Later in my life I travelled to Hong Kong and Taiwan, New York, Las Vegas, Dominican Republic, Mexico, Cuba, London, U.K., Italy, Holland, Switzerland, Venice, Monaco, Germany, Vatican, Spain, French Riviera, Belgium, Canada, Montreal, and Quebec. I have a few more countries on my bucket list and hope to resume my travels after 2020 covid-19 pandemic.

CHAPTER 12

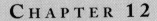

Moving On

My husband and I met in 1969, when I was seventeen and he was eighteen. It so happened, that his aunt and my Aunt Connie were friends. Every so often, his aunt would visit our house and spend a weekend with my aunt. Joey as he was commonly known to us would come by on a Sunday night, to pick her up and drive her home. Upon reaching his eighteenth birthday, his mom, bought him an older model Fiat and I guess it was also used to run errands. Usually, he would stop at the house and wait outside in his car for his aunt, but one day he decided to honk his horn. Ma being strict and straightforward did not like this and asked him to come inside. She told him that it is only proper to come and get his aunt inside. He apologized, but at the same time, noticed me and my sister, who was two years younger than me, inside the house. While the adults continued their conversation, he started chatting to us. The next time he came to pick his aunt up, he brought his friend with him and a mutual friendship developed with all of us. Being so young, Ma would not let us run around with boyfriends, but as I mentioned before, she did not object to our friends visiting at home and if she thought we were hanging out with the wrong people, she would intervene.

The longer Ma got to know Joey, the more she took a liking to him. Our friendship lasted for about four years with Joey and his friend visiting at the house and hanging out with us. Sometimes we would not see them for months, but Ma would always inquire about Joey, and I would say "Ma I don't know where Joey is. Maybe he found himself a steady girlfriend", to which she would reply, "I like the boy, hope he found a good girl for himself". There was one time, when Joey asked Ma whether he could take my sister and I to a party in Greenpoint. This was the first time that Ma said "yes" to a request like this, but she gave him strict instructions to have us home by 12 midnight. Joey's car was not in tip top shape and almost always needed a push or a mechanic nearby. On this night, Joey and his friend fetched us for the party and promised Ma that he would have us home by midnight. The party went well, and I think his family was celebrating his cousin's 21st birthday party. At around 11:20 pm, we got ready to go home in time to meet our curfew. To our dismay the car would not start. Fortunately, there was a mechanic in the area who got it fixed. This delayed our time and we finally got home after 1 a.m. way after our curfew. Joey took us inside only to find Ma up and waiting. He apologized for not meeting our curfew but explained that he had car problems, to which Ma replied "Young man that is the oldest excuse in the book. If you cannot have my girls' home in time, you will not have my permission to take them out again". I think this put him off, because we did not see them for a long time after that.

After not hearing from Joey, I started dating other guys. My sister met her husband, at the age of eighteen, and Ma was clearly not happy with the relationship. She sent my sister to live with my Dad and Aunty Maggie in 9th Avenue Retreat. One night, while working at a bank in Woodstock, I ran into Joey at the train station. He was disembarking to go home while I was about to embark. We were happy to see each other and while the train and passengers had long time gone, we were chatting on the station. He asked me whether he could come and visit, and I said "yes". By this time, I was 21 and although still living in Ma's house, was at the age where I could make my own decisions. We had a steady relationship and after asking for Ma, Pa, Dad and his Mom's permission, we got married at the age of 23 in my case and 24 in his. By this time, my sister and her husband were already married with a three-year-old daughter.

With my sister and I having moved out of Ma's house, my three remaining sisters were still single, and still living with her. As the years went by and with all of us married and no longer living with her, she remained the matriarch of our family and the person we would run to for support and advise, not forgetting her willingness to babysit for us whenever we were in need. As we grew older and had our own families, we realized why Ma had to always be strict with us. After raising her six children, and later five granddaughters it was certainly not easy. I will always love and appreciate her for what she did for us. By this time, all my aunties and uncles were married with their own families. Aunt Sarah was married with three children. Uncle John was married with two children, and Uncle Dan was married with one daughter. Aunt Veronica was also married with one daughter.

Aunt Connie fell in love with a "white" British immigrant (Bill). The two met in 1971 at a factory where they were employed. This factory was known as TEJ in Steenberg, known to manufacture hosiery, knitted jerseys, and socks. Bill was a Machine Minder and Connie was a Supervisor. The two started dating at a time when the "Immorality Act" made it a crime for a White person to have any sexual contact with a person of another race, and the "Prohibition of the mixed marriages act" and "The group areas act" which forbade people of one population group to live in a residential area reserved for another group. Despite the law that made it impossible for them to marry and the risk that they would be detected, they continued to be lovers. Often Aunt Connie and Bill had to dodge police raids. Luckily, they were never caught. If caught they would have faced a prison sentence of at least six years. Ma knowing what this type of relationship could mean for her daughter was totally against it and would not have Bill visit at home. Pa, however, was more laidback and welcomed Bill when Ma was not at home. The two would often share a drink together. This type of relationship would not last in South Africa; Connie and Bill decided to leave the country and settle in England, where they got married and had two daughters. After ten years in England, Bill accepted a job in Canada and relocated with his family.

When Aunt Connie left the country, I was twenty years old but even at that age I was devastated. Aunt Connie was torn between her love for us and her future with Bill. I am sure if things were different in South Africa, she would never have immigrated to another country. My second youngest sister was thirteen at the time; she thought of Aunt Connie as Mom ever since our Mom passed away when she was only three; she was heartbroken when Aunt Connie left. She told me many years later, that for the longest time she cried herself to sleep after Aunt Connie left. When Aunt Connie left in 1972, Ma still did not have a landline. This did not stop Aunt Connie from keeping in touch with the family by writing letters and sending pictures of her children. Ma in turn would frame the pictures and place it on the piano for all to see. I remember when we got a landline almost five years after Aunt Connie left, she was able to call home and the first time we heard her voice again, it was amazing!

In 1989, Joey and I decided to immigrate to Canada with our two sons who were thirteen and eight at the time. When I told Ma that we were leaving to settle in Canada, she was sad yet happy at the thought that her daughter (Aunt Connie) would have family in Canada. Aunt Connie and I were once again re-united in a different country, where she welcomed us in Canada and went out of her way to help us start a new life in a new country. South Africa's Apartheid Laws broke families and communities apart and caused irreparable damage for most families. When Joey and I left the country, South Africa's Apartheid Laws were still in place, therefore it was important for us to provide a better life for our kids, free of Apartheid. Aunt Connie, at the time of me writing this book (2020), has two daughters, six grandchildren and three great-grandchildren. Together with my two sons, Ma and Pa's offspring is expanding rapidly in Canada. Sadly, Aunt Connie passed away in 2006. Currently, Bill is still alive at an age of ninety-one. These are my family who together, played a part in shaping our future. I will forever be grateful to Wilhelmina and Daniel Joel McDuma (Ma and Pa) for keeping my sisters and I together, in a stable environment and providing all the love and attention, that all the motherless children need in this world. There are many orphaned children across the world, and I hope that one day, we will come up with a solution to give our future generation, a better chance in life.

THE END

My husband Joe and I, with my sons Justin and Ryan

Printed in the United States
By Bookmasters